# THE
# CREATION
## A LETTER

Dearest Maggie.
This book will give you
some idea what a blessing
you are to us and why
we love you so much.

Nana and Papa Bill
June 2, 2012

# THE
# CREATION
## A LETTER

**Outskirts Press, Inc.**
**Denver, Colorado**

The Creation: A Letter
All Rights Reserved.
Copyright © 2011 Donald Jordan
Watercolorist: Donald Jordan
v4.0

Outskirts Press, Inc.
http://www.outskirtspress.com

PB ISBN: 978-1-4327-7060-0
HB ISBN: 978-1-4327-7487-5

Library of Congress Control Number: 2011902255

Outskirts Press and the "OP" logo are trademarks belonging to Outskirts Press, Inc.

PRINTED IN THE UNITED STATES OF AMERICA

A grandchild is a blessing. Seven are God's bountiful gift. It is important to me, and I believe urgent in our modern American culture, that my four youngest grasp something of a kind and generous world view; and that the three older will be encouraged to stay the course. If you like this little book I hope you will share it with your children; better still, that it will inspire you to write your own letter. This would fulfill our purpose.

Dear Children:

Your mother came into the world like a ray of light, black hair, blue eyes, a little miracle of creation. When I looked into her startled and wondering eyes, when I examined her perfectly made little feet and body, I saw the hand of God.

How, I wondered, could I protect her from all the disappointments and difficulties she would suffer? How could I defend her against pain and disillusion? How could I help form and shape her to withstand the inevitable assaults on her character, her goodness?

All through life we struggle with ambition, with material desires, with the hope that we will be noticed by the world. I have come to believe that above all, love is our most significant achievement. It is the thing that makes us truly human and truly divine. All our worldly ambitions and accomplishments ultimately pale against the power of love. However instinctive love might seem, it does not develop naturally. Like faith, the reverence for love is a gift of the spirit, apart from the temptations of the flesh. It must be learned and cultivated. Often we don't fully grasp until later in life that to love and be loved is the only legacy we leave that lasts. How could I instill this concept in your mother? For the first dozen or so years of her life

# THE CREATION

I thought about writing her a letter such as this one; but the years pass quickly and the influences we had on her personality and her convictions were formed by word and deed. So now I write to you, beloved grandchildren, this little message of things I believe, hoping it will be a light to you as your mother has been a light to me.

Know this: I will always love you, no matter what. Love is self-manifesting. It does not have to be returned. It is never divided, instead it multiplies itself. Many flowers proliferate by casting their seed. So too love grows stronger and more vigorous when it is freely given.

Love is not just a feeling, it is a decision. If you consciously inject it into the worst situations, into the most infuriating actions of others, it may not change what happens in your lives, but it will dramatically change the way you carry what happens in your minds and hearts. Love is an attitude that is learned, practiced and outreaching. It is a decision.

My own parents were not very demonstrative people. We knew they loved us, but seldom heard the expression of their love in words. From the day your mother was born we said, "I love you." Consequently, one of the first strings of words she put together was "I love you." At first it came out "Ibechu," then "Iuvu," and in time "I love you." Love lives in our hearts but it should live on our lips, too. Put it in your vocabulary. Say it to your brother, your sister. The more you say "I love you," the more natural, the more meaningful it will become. The expression of love should be a facet of your character. Without it, what is the motivation for honesty, generosity, and compassion? Perhaps it is not the cure-all for all the world's ills; yet, if person-to-person, neighbor-by-neighbor, nation-by-nation we could learn to care for and respect one another, what a transformation mankind would witness!

So much of life depends on how we view things, and how we view things depends on the attitude we choose. I don't believe lasting joy can be found in mere circumstances. Things can make us happy for a while, but happiness fades as quickly as circumstances change. I believe only inner joy can be sustaining.

Each day when you awaken, think of some little thing that will bring you pleasure. This may be no more than walking with a friend, doing something for others, reading a poem. No matter how bleak the day before you might appear, you can choose to seek something every morning that will bring light into your lives.

As a middle child I was a serious young man, seeking, vulnerable, trying to find my place in the world. I wanted to be wealthy and famous, and most of all to make a difference. I wanted to contribute something significant, I wanted to be noticed. I believe one of the strongest human needs is the need to be appreciated.

But you will not always be appreciated. You won't

always feel a part of things. If you choose to rise above seeking approval of your peers, if you choose not to be ordinary, you must expect to be attacked. The world seldom looks with favor upon those who are different.

I believe that with love as your foundation you can learn the following principles which will bring joy into your lives:

Be kind always, toward all God's creatures, whether human or animal. Your grandmother is an example of one who embodies the gift of kindness. Nothing pleases her more than to take bouquets of flowers to a nursing home or a bag of groceries to some less fortunate family. She has the gift of service, and never expects anything in return. Her remedy for a down day is to do some little thing for others. Make kindness shine in your actions and responses. It will never fail to reward you.

Be compassionate. Never be afraid to cry. One day I came across a tragedy that had just occurred. A seven or eight year old boy had been killed by a car. It tore my heart to see his skull cracked open, but just as anguishing was to see the man sitting on the steps across the street with his head down in his hands. How horrible it must have been to have run over the child, what he must suffer for years to come! I was just sick for him. Compassion for the pain and suffering for another person, for a defenseless animal — even for your enemy — can be learned if you consider what your own feelings would be under their circumstances. Your culture will teach you to shield yourselves from wounds and trouble. It will teach you that others are put here for your own use. Resist the temptation to protect your sensitivities with a shield of indifference and toughness.

Practice generosity always. It doesn't matter how little or how much you have, it matters only that you are generous with what you have. As meager as my family's possessions were, my mother and father somehow managed always to find a few dollars for a friend who had suffered some crippling loss. With money, as with time and compassion, be generous. Generosity is the fruit from which you will draw nourishment. The joy of the gift comes back to the giver. Don't ask or expect recognition. You will never exceed the grace and love that has been given to you.

Express gratitude for everything, however small it might be. An attitude of appreciation will bring light into your day. Your words of thanks are just as beneficial to you as they are to the person who has been kind to you.

As much as you can, forgive. My mother, your great grandmother Wylma, was the most forgiving person I have ever known. People could slight her, ridicule her, take things from her and she refused to hold it against them. Sometimes we thought she was too forgiving. I wish now that I could be more like her. I confess I am not very forgiving when someone lies or breaks his word.

To me the most important character trait is responsibility. You must always take responsibility for your promises, your word, and your actions. Whatever you say you will do, do it. You should blame the world, your environment, your culture, your peers for nothing. Always you have the power of choice. You can choose to live your life responsibly, regardless of what others choose. In our culture today, we are so accustomed to unnecessary lies and irresponsible behavior it is difficult to trust anyone. I believe disregard for truth and responsibility damages our sense of self-love, and it is self-love that helps us develop sensitivity toward others and their pain. Don't let your word fail you. It is your best currency in an environment of moral bankruptcy.

Along with responsibility comes honesty. Try not to lie, but if you must, do it for the protection of others. Try to see the other person's point of view, be willing to compromise in an argument, but never compromise your beliefs, your faith, or your conscience. Once in seventh grade I couldn't remember the answers to a couple of questions on a test. I slipped a note to the girl next to me asking the answers. The teacher saw this, confiscated the note and stood staring at me for several cold seconds. She never said a word. She didn't have to. I wanted to shrink under my desk. And why do I remember this incident of so long ago? Because I was beginning to understand that winning by cheating or plagiarizing is ultimately failure. Every individual is born with a sense of what is right and what is wrong. Do not allow your morals to be diluted. If you choose a high standard of morality you may be ridiculed. But remember, it will be you, not others, who are responsible for your actions and your decisions. Honesty is your shield against self-corruption.

And remember that money is important, but has limits. It will buy neither love, health nor friendship. The desire for financial freedom is inherent in everyone. I doubt that there is a living person who doesn't desire the independence and security of wealth. It is the key to many doors, not the least of which is the freedom for creative contribution. I don't expect you to disregard the appeal of material things, only to keep it in perspective. Be a good steward of all your resources — money, time, and gifts. Save some part of your earnings. With money it is better to be austere than extravagant. Guard your storehouse responsibly; try to increase it a little year by year in preparation for old age. At the same time, do not revere money. It is a means but not an end. In the world today the hunger for material possessions has become destructive. Treat anything you have as a valuable asset to be managed but not loved. Be a good steward, compassionate toward those less fortunate.

Finally, love others. This is not always easy. It isn't always easy even to like people. They can be mean, obnoxious, and spiteful. To love those who revile and hate you often seems humanly impossible. You can learn to love them anyway. An attitude of love, of responsibility, of compassion and generosity doesn't come naturally. It must be cultivated. It must stand strong against a popular culture which will mock your values and your convictions.

We must realize that a joyful life comes from the spirit, whose evidences are kindness and service to others.

I believe these fruit of the spirit must be understood and embraced. I believe the more this spirit grows the more we develop the capacity for true joy. I believe that without love, none of the other facets of human goodness will reach our hearts. I admit I have failed over and over, but perhaps even my failures will help me offer some small light for you to follow.

So if none other, this is the gift I leave you and your children and your children's children: the eternal legacy of the love of one man who was part of bringing you into life.

As a small boy I walked from our home to church. It was only a few blocks, and in those days no one thought anything of children walking and playing in the streets. On birthdays we would bring our pennies to Sunday School and drop them in a jar. As we did so the class would sing a little rhyme:

> Donald's had a birthday, we are glad.
> Let us see how many he has had.
> As we count the pennies we are told,
> One, two, three, four, five,
> Yes, the pennies say he's five years old.

# A LETTER

At some time during the year these birthday pennies were gathered together with other contributions and sent to missionaries in the field to feed the hungry and the poor. We learned early the principles of helping those in need.

The contribution of these pennies was no little thing for us. My father worked night and day to make ends meet. By ten or eleven I had a paper route. Back then papers were delivered by boys on bicycles. My route was hard, up steep hills with houses set far back. Bitter, cold, rainy mornings were grueling and scary. Sometimes I was sick, nervous, on edge. Several times I was attacked by packs of dogs. But on my trusted Schwinn I pushed on anyway. With my earnings I bought my own shoes and haircuts. The cruel demands of this work taught me self-assurance, but it was a hard way to learn. As I grew older, when the offering plate was passed I seldom forgot that there were kids less fortunate than I.

Love of God and of one another is the very essence of God's message to us. It is difficult to understand why in America today those who believe this message of love are so often reviled. It's true that in the name of God men have done vile things, yet thousands of schools, orphanages, hospitals, food banks and water sources have been built by those who believe for those who do not. One does not seek God through the world or its people. For the peace of His love we cannot rely on worldly circumstances or conditions.

Once when your mother was small she was reluctant

to go down the hall to her dark room for some book or toy. Her mother encouraged her. "You'll be okay. God will go with you."

She had almost reached her room when she came running back. "I want God <u>and</u> you to go with me!"

In her mind she needed to see God, she sought physical evidence. And I suspect such a need follows us all. We want God <u>and</u> the world.

I wish I could protect you from all your pain, your hurts, your disappointments. Even with the best of attitudes, the purest world view, you will suffer rejection and loneliness. Even your friends and fellow believers will attack you. You'll be slighted, you'll be hurt in love, you'll be sad. You will meet people who will seem more attractive, charming, or popular than you, and you'll envy them. Remember that it's better not to pretend to be what you are not, it is better to be quiet than to assume false airs. You'll fear many things: the death of your loved ones, the destruction of the world, the possibility that you will never see your dreams fulfilled. One of the most difficult of human experiences is to realize at last that our lives will never be as we thought they would be. I wish I could protect you from the pain and fear you are bound to face. I can only emphasize that you should never weigh yourselves on the scales of circumstances and environment. Self-esteem, which every mind and heart seeks, comes not from the acceptance of others and pride in your accomplishments, but from the capacity to love: to love others and to love yourself as a child of love's Creator.

When my grandmother — your great-great grandmother Lula — a teacher of Latin, married, she forsook academia to live a bitterly hard farm life. The struggle for food, clothing, and access to medicine was unending, hours of toil from before dawn until well after dark; yet nearly all this generation found time for church and revivals, and more importantly, just as my father and mother did, they found a few dollars to give to those in greater need.

# THE CREATION

Despite their hardships, they were happy. I, too, was happy on my grandmother's Alabama farm. My best weekends and holidays were those during which I climbed high into cotton hills in the cotton barn, rode mules bareback (despite the painful chaffing of my bottom), and gathered eggs from the hen house. In summer the fields were breathtaking with acres of peach blossoms, and the wonderful smells of canning lifted our spirits. In winter the house was cold and we buried ourselves beneath thick feather quilts. Split log fires hissed in the hearth and we had to rotate our bodies, warming front and back alternately.

At the edge of their garden was a huge pecan tree. Each year, but for a rare poor season, this tree dropped large, healthy nuts. These were gathered for their own use and for candies and cakes to sell. It was one of the little ways Grandmother Lula supplemented their income. The pecans were harvested and shelled with handheld crackers and picks. It was slow and tedious work, as many aspects of their lives were. My brother and I would climb high into the tree, venture out onto the limbs and shake the nuts down. Though you may never experience such a bucolic scene as this, I hope you can share your great-great-grandmother's reverence for the land.

Next to grandmother's was my aunt's farm where there was a hillside pine grove. Underneath was little vegetation, only a thick mat of pine straw. I would walk down the lane to this grove, lie on the straw with my head resting against a tree, and dream the dreams of a young boy painting pictures of his future. Birds, squirrels and hawks accepted me, and the sun dappling down through the pines made me doze. It was a beautiful time which I shall always remember.

Not far from the pine grove was a cold water stream called Big Branch. Here the water ran down an old sawmill road, shallow, rushing over sparkling pebbles. We'd undress, wade up the road, choosing our steps carefully, then dip into the deep pool formed by tree trunks and branches. The water was icy but our forages to Big Branch were more exciting than any city pool could have been.

My grandfather, your great-great-grandfather, whom I never knew, died of pneumonia at an early age, leaving three small boys for grandmother to raise. She fought to survive, fought to keep the land. She was a tough and outspoken woman, who stood strong against all assaults. Forthright and courageous, she was blunt and untiringly loyal to her family and her responsibilities. There is a story about how one night she heard a noise out around her barnyard. In the darkness she crept to the window and saw the silhouette of a man trying to steal her mule. She took her pistol and fired one shot into the oak tree next to him. He dropped the rope and fled. To our knowledge no one ever attempted to steal from her again.

To singlehandedly manage a farm while rearing three boys was harshly demanding of grandmother. Perhaps it was <u>her</u> genes which drove me to rise on black cold mornings, dress, climb onto my bicycle and hurry off to deliver papers to homes where nearly everybody else slept. There were other boys my age doing the same, and maybe we were some of the last ten- and twelve-year-olds who had to work so hard to make our own way.

This kind of self-reliance may be difficult for you to learn. We live in a world which doesn't encourage it. I fear that our great nation is becoming a state of failed socialism. Many believe it is the government's job to take care of us. The government's job is as much as possible to stay out of our lives. To turn everything over to the handful of men and women who make up the laws of our country is in time to transfer us into a dictatorship, and under dictatorship the individual means little.

Liberal minds are writing America's finest hours out of history. Traditional values and tried and tested convictions are being abandoned. The values we hold precious were not easily won. Our ancestors — <u>your</u> ancestors — fought in every American war beginning with the American Revolution. They believed in patriotism, love of country, love of God. They believed in self-reliance, stout-heartedness, trustworthiness. They wanted to be left alone to work out their own lives, always keeping in mind the common good. They asked and expected nothing from anyone, especially the government. They cared for their neighbors and no matter how poor they were they could always find a way to help those in need. They had to watch every penny, but would cheat no one. They would have been appalled at the idea of a handout. Their doors were left open, their windows never locked. While their feelings ran deep, they seldom expressed them. They persevered and hoped to give something to the world, not merely take from it.

It saddens me to think that you are growing up in an environment where there are Americans who would destroy everything America stands for. No American is proud of the arrogance, the avidity, the hypocrisy which is a cancer to our spirit. But without democracy, liberty, free enterprise, and especially the spiritual and moral foundation upon which our founding fathers laid the cornerstones of our society, we will cease to exist as a distinct nation with distinct people. There are those who would like to see America brought to her knees.

We may well be suffering the end of our nation as we have known it. The concept of selfless and sacrificial love appears to be gasping its last breath; personal interest comes ahead of all else, regardless of its effect on others; our role models are not great statesmen and thinkers who revere their country and its people, but celebrities whose thirst for admiration and power is insatiable. We do not trust our neighbor, let alone a stranger. We are skeptical about God, therefore have no real moral anchor. Too many people choose to avoid any real emotional involvement. More and more we elect not to sacrifice ourselves to any cause which fails to provide personal security and success. I'm afraid that your heaven will consist of gratifications invented by men, not the heaven of grace and forgiveness; that in institutions of higher learning free expression will be denied to those who dare speak of or read about faith. America looks nothing like it did fifty, thirty or even twenty years ago. People see little to believe in.

More and more we are challenged to decide between a loving Creator and the theory of evolution. Either every individual is created for a purpose, or we are no more than the product of natural selection. The secular mind cannot comprehend that for some there is an awareness which comes not from the intellect but from a supernatural sense. Non-believers will tell you that heaven is invented by men who want to believe they will live forever; believers will tell you it is this spiritual awareness that assures them of the reality of God.

If because of your faith you are accused of stupidity or weak-mindedness, you might consider a few of the great men who believed in God. Sir Isaac Newton was a legendary scientist, astronomer and mathematician; Friedrich Wilhelm Herschel was the inventor of the modern telescope; James Maxwell was a Scottish physicist who unlocked many of the secrets of life; Eric Van Fromm was the father of space exploration; the complexity of life and of physics led Albert Einstein, one of the most brilliant minds of all times, to believe there must be divine intelligence behind it. If these scientists predated our so-called modern enlightenment, consider this: Anthony Flew, known as "the world's most notorious atheist," came to the conclusion that Einstein was right about a deity — in

2004! Nevertheless, if you believe as these great thinkers believed, "you must have the courage to have your wisdom regarded as stupidity . . . you must have the courage to suffer the contempt of the sophisticated world." As Antonin Scalia, Justice of the Supreme Court, continues, "God assumed from the beginning that the wise of the world would view Christians as fools . . . and He has not been disappointed."

Remember: faith is not about believing you will be shielded from every assault and trouble; it is not about believing you will always be materially blessed. There is nothing in Biblical theology that promises immunity to tribulation, or guarantees any kind of earthly reward. To walk in a Godly attitude is ten times more difficult than to be seduced by the appeal of a secular world. Faith is believing that you will be given the grace to accept whatever happens. This is one of our most troubling challenges. Painful as life's trials might be, sometimes the most difficult ones ultimately prove to be beneficial to us.

Despite the secularization of America I believe it remains the world's finest nation. When I look at the noble and courageous foundation of our heritage, my heart swells with pride. The first great revolutionary fight for independence, the brave frontiersmen who gambled their lives in quest of land, the generations of soldiers and inventors and ordinary people who risked everything to make their country strong — we must not forget this heritage. There are still young men and women who believe with all their hearts that in the human spirit there is something more than lust for material possessions and self-interest. There are still those who believe life on earth is not merely about possessions, pleasure and position. There are still those who are willing to risk their lives for strangers, who know there are worse things than death, who have faith in dignity and compassion and prayer. There are still those who believe everyone is endowed by their Creator not merely with the rights of life and liberty but with the freedom of choice — to believe or not believe, to love or not love, to give or not give. Whenever a tsunami strikes far off shore or a hurricane batters our own coastline, Americans respond with unequaled outpouring of compassion and generosity.

Never believe that America is a mean-spirited and arrogant nation. Never believe that America wants to use its super power to enforce its will on other nations. More Americans have died for the cause of liberty and freedom on foreign soil than any other peoples. In our capitalistic society there is bound to be greed and corruption. Don't look at that tiny segment of politicians and entertainers and money manipulators. For what it has stood for and fought for, America has nothing to be ashamed of. Be proud of her.

Your generation has more challenges and choices than any before you. The computer highway provides you with unparalleled access to information. You have at your fingertips resources to be the most knowledgeable generation in history; yet, misguided choices can lead you into a state of spiritual stagnation in which you have nothing to rely on but material <u>things</u>. I encourage you to trust in your God-given ambitions and the courage to do what you believe to be right. For anything in life that comes free we usually pay with a little of our dignity and our spirit. I ask you to turn your lives over to no one in this world, but to try to use your time and your gifts to make life a little better for those who follow.

What you choose to believe or not believe about God will impact your view of life. How you live, how you react, and how you treat others touches the lives around you. It is up to each one of us to decide what kind of missionary we will be. My grandmother's generation, my parents' generation and my own generation believed our contributions would make life a little better for our children. Now many of us fear that for our children and our grandchildren we leave less hope than any past generation.

I encourage you to mine your heritage of self-resolve, to believe in yourself and as little as possible ask others to help you carry your load. I encourage you to try to love people. Try to use your minds, your determination, your vision, and your faith to leave the world a little more than you take from it. Every man and woman can make a difference.

# THE CREATION

At age two your mother was in her first dance program. Through the months of practice she was always the dancer who led the line out onto the stage. At the last minute another girl was put in front of her. Not to be outdone, on the night of the review, as the girls came out in their little hula costumes, your mother simply wriggled around the lead girl and assumed command of the line. The audience was delighted.

Even before this, at eighteen months, when your grandmother was teaching your mother to swim, your mother would allow no assistance from the side of the pool. She jumped in on her own and swam like a mermaid to whomever waited for her.

When your mother was in the first grade she brought home an invitation for parents to attend a play. She got the time wrong and when we reached the school the play was over. As we walked late into her classroom she looked up and burst into tears. It was a moment that shot arrows of love and protectiveness into our hearts. How essential we were to her! How much she wanted to shine before us! Someday when you are old enough, you will learn that family is about the most important thing you'll have in this world.

One night we were riding through "the jungle" at The Eagle, our country place, looking for lions and tigers, elephants and bears. We backed into a low-limbed tree and down came a showerfall of Daddy Longlegs, those silly looking spiders that tickle but don't bite. Your mother and her cousin on back of the truck screamed and stamped and thrashed. The insects were harmless but the accidental invasion was shocking. Does this explain why to this day your mother panics at a close encounter with a spider?

By the time she was six months old we were reading to her. She loved all books, especially stories like *Jack and the Beanstalk*, and *Little Red Riding Hood*. Perhaps it was the element of adventure and danger which appealed to her. And nursery rhymes — it was amazing how much she grasped. Before age two she could recite verbatim dozens of them. "Wucy Wocket wost her pocket . . ." Perhaps this was why at an early age she began to write her own stories which she stapled into little books. I hope you will also write down your thoughts and feelings. Recording your daily experiences and your impressions, however brief, will someday be of great value to you. Discipline yourselves to writing a paragraph, even just a sentence each day.

And read, read, read. Your mind will never reach its full potential through films, games, or popular music. It is the written word which will most likely open your eyes to your own possibilities. As a teenager I read John Locke and Plato and Charles Lamb. The books which most influenced my life were Charles Sheldon's *In His Steps*, C.S. Lewis' *The Screwtape Letters*, and Lloyd C. Douglas' *Magnificent Obsession*, which describes the concept of doing for others in secret. I encourage you to read these. My favorite novels were the stories by Albert Payson Terhune, Dickens' *A Tale of Two Cities* and Eliot's *Silas Marner*. My romantic heart was touched by the Bronte sisters, by Evans' *St. Elmo,* and much later by Pasternak's *Doctor Zhivago.* Books are experiences. Digest them thoroughly. They help shape your thoughts, your personality. Avoid nothing, but always weigh the truths of what you read.

Enjoy music, learn to dance, exercise — these are gifts free for everyone. Develop a sense of humor. Don't be afraid to laugh. During the most difficult times try to find something to smile about. Bring humor into your view of the world. Try to tell yourselves that despite your troubles, you can find a reason to laugh at yourselves.

Learn to be outgoing. As a child and young man I was shy. Your mother learned to reach out not only from me and her mother but from her older sister, who taught her at only a few months of age to wriggle around the floor like sizzling bacon, to make a happy face, a sad or surprised face. Her sister influenced her personality with prayer and drama. Learn to be bold and convivial before other people.

And live life creatively. There is great value in individual expression, even if that expression is never shared. You have the power to create your own world, to discover yourselves. Try to turn every circumstance, good and bad, into something meaningful. Respect the wealth of information modern technology offers. Listen to the wise and experienced, but listen, too, to your own minds. In many ways we are all alone. Don't be afraid to experience everything you can. Try to love whatever you do, always.

# A LETTER

Work hard, never be a slacker, never give up, never quit. Some days you won't feel like dragging yourselves out of bed. Get up anyway. You won't feel like singing. Sing anyway. You won't love or even like people. Try to remember that they are created in the same Image as you.

The grace of God's Spirit is within all who wish to draw from it. I believe in the morality of the soul which tells us what we should and shouldn't do. I believe those born in the most difficult circumstances can distinguish right from wrong. If this law of the spirit ever fails you, if you don't have a clear answer, apply this rule: do nothing you wouldn't wish others to see. If you err, don't let remorse consume you. Forgive and be forgiven, then let your mistakes go.

❧

Does one life matter? I believe one individual can make a difference. In so many ways you'll stand alone, but you must remain strong in what you believe, tough against the attacks on your view of right and wrong. I hope you will never settle for the mediocre. People will answer your compassion with indifference, generosity with self-indulgence, love with doubt, responsibility with scorn. So habituated is our society to lies and manipulation that a good and honest person is often suspect.

I've told you that as a young man I was inspired to make great contributions. I wanted to be a voice in the world, I wanted to change lives. Never did I feel I was granted the opportunity to reach my potential. Very likely, my vision was beyond my capabilities. Ideals should be encouraged, but one must learn to expect less. I have come to the conclusion that if one can touch just one or two lives, if one can strive to make the world a little better place, if one can help others less fortunate from time to time, he has been given a reason to live.

You may never have your name in lights, you may never have a highway or school or theater named after you. But with God's help you can create events in your life which will be positive and character forming. What happens, happens. We cannot change the past, we can only choose our attitude toward circumstances in our lives.

You are the hope for the future. Dare to be different. Don't follow the hordes. Abuse, inhumanity, and aggression have always been with us. You see it in the cult of celebrity, in corporate greed, in the hypocrisy of world leaders. It has never been obvious evil, the bold face of wickedness or sensual appetite which most damages us. It's the quietly persuasive, the undercurrents of suggestion which steal upon us like a thief in the night.

Though it may not seem so to you now, our time on earth is brief. Live as though what you say and do will have a lasting effect on those who follow. Be a good steward of what you have, not what you wish to have. Practice enjoying the little things that come every day instead of waiting for the big things which usually do not. Appreciate the gift of reason and the power of decision. Embrace the spirit of love which continues after life on earth and links past and present and future.

Mother Teresa of Calcutta was a follower of Jesus who gave her life in service to the sick, to the poor and orphaned. Here are her words: People are often unreasonable and self-centered. Forgive them anyway. If you are kind, people may accuse you of ulterior motives. Be kind anyway. If you are honest, people may cheat you. Be honest anyway. If you find happiness, people may be jealous. Be happy anyway. The good you do today may be forgotten tomorrow. Do good anyway. Give the world the best you have and it may never be enough. Give your best anyway. For you see, in the end, it is between you and God. It was never between you and them anyway.

✍⌀

Whatever others may do, be true to yourselves. Never tire of doing good, of doing what is right, and try to be optimistic and positive. You may walk through a valley, but if you keep your eyes lifted you'll see the mountain top. If you don't see it, keep on anyway, know it's there. When bad things happen to you, you can spend your life looking back, or you can choose to look forward. Regretting what might have been erodes the soul. I know this from experience.

Defend the weak, but never use your strength to bully. Believe little of what you read and hear. Remember that many of those who assume responsibility for bringing you news of the world bring you instead their personal agendas. My generation was taught to honor and respect not the political leaders but the offices they held. The political parties were not that far apart. They had mutual respect for one another and shared commitment to the good of the nation. Never before in my lifetime have we experienced such hatred as each political party now has for the other. Don't let yourselves be manipulated into despising those who don't agree with you.

Remember that love, generosity, kindness and compassion aren't material things you can touch, taste and smell. They are treasures of the spirit, set apart and unblemished.

I encourage you to listen, and when you speak, make certain you have something to say. Guard your tongue. It can be a vicious flame or poultice for an aching wound. It can be a pure sonnet of love or rotten with deceit. It can mend or rip apart.

And if you have a friend, respect and value him or her. When I was sixteen my father became critically ill and I assumed responsibility for our family. What lonely years followed! A friend would have made all the difference. But be careful. A broken friendship can be very painful. Make certain those you choose to befriend closely want an intimate friendship.

Respect and treasure your own bodies. Don't abuse them. Don't allow others to violate them. Throughout your life, from the time you are young until you grow old, you'll be told that your bodies are to be used, experimented with, that pleasures of the flesh in every form are natural. Be careful of how much of this you listen to. Remember that people, even your own peers — especially your own peers — may use you. A moment's passion can bring a lifetime of consequences. This doesn't mean you should avoid passion. It, too, is a gift which can bring joy. But don't allow it to overwhelm you. The things we over-indulge may make our most precious blessings ordinary. Set an example of dignity for those around you. Your failures can cause others to fail. Don't cave in under pressure to make yourselves acceptable.

I encourage you to have fun. Life is a gift. It is not intended to be gloomy. There is the opportunity for joy everywhere. Smile. Laugh. Practice a sense of humor and it'll become second nature to you.

And be sure to make room for quiet time. This can be anywhere, in any prayerful moment — just a few minutes each day to get away from the rush and splash of the world. If you can, walk in the woods. Nature has a special song for us all. Be sensitive to everything, listen. Let the Holy Spirit walk with you there.

~~

When your mother was a young girl she loved The Eagle. It isn't as spectacular as the colorful North Georgia mountains or the coastal salt marshes to the east. But it's a little gem of creation, ours to use for a while. I don't believe we as individuals ever truly own nature. We may take possession of it for a time, but sky, streams, trees and flowers are gifts to be savored by everyone.

Here is where your mother learned to drive a golf cart, cast a spinner reel, run and play with our sable and white collie. In a great sweet gum we built a three-tiered tree house. She could climb steps up into its crotch, from here ascend to the first level, then on twisting steps to the second, and finally to the loftiest perch of all, high into the branches where she could look out over the woods and lakes — all solid, sturdy platforms with guard rails. For many years she and her friends glided like butterflies to this treasured tree house where they lived among the leaves, spinning out their stories and their plans. Many years later your mother gave me a little book about a re-lationship between a little boy and a tree. The title is *The Giving Tree* by Shel Silverstein, and my heart will never fail to be touched when I read it.

At age five your mother lost a fishing rod in a lake. She had laid it on the pier and a big fish took it away. Five years later, at age ten, she was fishing on this same pier and through some extraordinary trick of fate she fished it out again.

Often we engaged in hide and seek along the hillside trails. One group of her girlfriends would go ahead, pick up sticks and arrange arrows indicating their direction. The second group would come behind, find the arrows and make turns as indicated. It was a game of mystery, intrigue and discovery.

One of the things your mother liked best was to go to the old country store just a mile or so from The Eagle. Here she would find little treasures — something special to eat, unusual candies, rings, sparklers, gigantic sunglasses. As a small boy I had done the same. The country stores I liked best were way out from my grandmother's farm, usually on crossroads, wood buildings sided with Coca-Cola and tobacco signs, heated by pot-bellied wood stoves and jammed with bridles and plow points and trace chains, sewing materials and cloth for the ladies and for the children water guns and caps and jaw breakers. The odors were tantalizing, of salted smokehouse meat and molasses and pecans; of dusty wood floors and kerosene lamps and of corn and cotton. The sounds were special, too, of rain on tin roofs, of the hum of voices and ungreased wagon wheels and cowbells in the pastures. I have observed that you, too, love the old country store, with its B-B games and slingshots and candy cigarettes. The country store was part of the old rural scene where farmers and field hands found a moment to talk, to have a cool drink.

From me, from your grandmother, and from your mother and father, I hope you will learn to love and respect the land, even whatever is abnormal and unsightly. If you walk the trails and firebreaks of The Eagle without observing closely you'll probably see nothing extraordinary. The Piedmont-Coastal Plains region of our state doesn't compare with the glacial lakes and snow-shrouded mountains of the American north, or the splendid white beaches of the south. But if you open your minds and hearts to the messages of nature, you'll discover that the miracles of creation are everywhere. You'll experience a reverence for earth's beauty which may make it difficult to believe that all nature's treasures occur by natural coincidence.

Follow the beaver. From mud and sticks he can build an all but impenetrable dam, much more efficiently than human hands. With an instinct for engineering he might construct a diversion dam at the precise elevation to equalize pressure. Follow the birds. Some will fly three thousand miles, then return to the exact nesting site where they were born to raise their own young. During the summer the pea-sized brain of the chickadee develops "place cells" which allow it to hide and later find thousands of seeds.

Follow the spider and notice the intricate strength and resilience of their webs. Spider silk is the strongest fiber in the world, a hundred times stronger than steel. Follow the honeybee. When the bee discovers a source of food he will return to the hive and through a series of turns, his waggle dance, communicate the navigational direction for his coworkers to fly to the nectar source.

We think of trees as inanimate objects, but can they speak? There is evidence that rhizomes, a network of filaments in the forest floor, form a communications system whereby trees warn others of swarming insects or approaching dangers. Is all this the phenomenal accidents of evolution or the work of loving design? You must walk, look, listen and decide for yourselves.

I don't believe we are given this precious and fragile earth to use and abuse at will, assuming it will be refurbished and recreated as needed. In 1993 I received perhaps the only public award I shall ever be given. It is the Georgia Department of Natural Resources' Forest Steward award that says in part, "Your stewardship practices leave a better world than you found to those who will follow." I hope someday it will truly be said that I have tried to leave a better world than I found.

I believe we are stewards of all we have been given and that we often fail in so many ways. I encourage you to remember the love of nature's Creator and to respect animals and plants with a sense of responsibility for all.

At The Eagle if you walk south from the cabin, you'll find an outcrop of boulders sloping down to wetlands where marsh mallows grow. Across the creek, a bog is home to spear-shaped palmettos and acres of fragile rain lilies. Here great white oaks are the patriarchs of the forest while red maple and wild blueberries sprinkle the understory. To the north an old stagecoach road shafts through, and on the lakes are great blue herons and sometimes an inland osprey. Two trees growing across each other stroke and massage high up, sounding like the rhythmic creaking of a porch swing. To the east is a waterfall, not a dramatic one, nevertheless a rush of clear spring water over rocks, cascading and swirling like young girls gossiping. It is amazing to watch a wood duck fly at a high speed right through the three-inch opening into a nesting box. In spring and fall a walk up and down the creek will give you a fresh view of honeysuckle growing high into the trees, of purple-staining American beautyberry and an occasional pocket of Queen Anne's Lace. These are some of the things you will discover.

I believe that love of country, not only for its natural beauty but for its people, its heart and soul, its diversity, its complexity of thought and feeling, is the only way we will avoid natural catastrophe. We must somehow return to the roots laid down by our ancestors — concern, compassion and protectiveness toward creation and toward others.

When men finally escaped earth's gravity and rocketed into the heavens, some of the Russian cosmonauts looked out upon the glorious universe and reported that they "could not find God anywhere," while several of America's astronauts were awestruck by the beauty of the seas and deserts, the mountains and valleys, the colors of a master Painter. We were given a Garden of Eden, yet it's a pity that in the name of economic development and the immigration of millions we are paving our land with asphalt and brick.

The miracles of creation are found not only in nature

but in friends, in brothers and sisters, in loved ones, in family. Most scientists insist that men evolved from a single cell amoeba. Yet modern technology tells us that a single cell can carry more data than all the volumes of the *Encyclopedia Britannica.* Could such life really have evolved from a primordial mass? This cannot explain the presence of the soul, which I believe lives in every human apart from any other animal and apart from circumstances, environment and learning.

The soul grows through sadness and sorrow and struggle. When I was a child I had a little white spaniel. We called her Frisky because she was such a frisky thing. As we romped and played together, I knew she loved me. Somehow she invaded a neighbor's trash can and ate chicken bones. Though we had little money, my parents rushed her to the veterinarian. I prayed she would live. When she died I felt angry that God hadn't heard me. I couldn't understand why He would take my friend away.

When my older brother was called into military service during the Korean War I felt frightened and alone. Most of our lives he had delighted in taunting and tormenting me, so I would have thought I would look forward to having a room alone at last. Instead, I wept. A part of my world collapsed.

All through life we experience pain and confusion and contradiction. Bitter as these are, they are part of shaping our world view, part of what we are to become, and part of preparing us to help others who are in pain.

Nature can be cruel, too. Tornadoes, forest fires, ice and snowstorms can obliterate entire communities, claiming dozens of lives. But for every cruel moment, nature sends us the promise of soft winds and sunshine. As the poet Shelley says, "If winter comes, can spring be far behind?"

Sometimes on cold winter mornings at The Eagle you can walk out and find thousands of fine webs spun across the ground. They are white and vary in size from about six to twelve inches. I don't know what kind of spiders make these, or even if they're made by spiders. The filaments are thin as cotton silk and intricately made, delicate to the touch. They are unlike frost which usually touches every tip of grass. Both burn away under the eastern dawn, both in their white beauty a brushstroke of creation caught only by the early riser who walks ahead of the rising sun.

Sometimes I'll look back to see my footprints on the icy canvas. These are my physical footprints which like the gauzy webs or filamentous frost will burn away. But I often wonder what kind of spiritual footprints I'll leave behind and how you might follow in them.

I've mentioned the paper route that I had at a young age. On my three- and four-hour paper delivering afternoons and Sunday mornings I saw the sunrise slowly backlighting the trees, stealing silently over the earth. I saw the glow of resurrection, the promise of awakening from sleep, the first stirrings of animals and birds. Sometimes my spirit was heavy with the ordeal before me, the long high hills, the brittle cold from which gloves and raincoats offered little protection. Sometimes my spirit was elated by the first daffodil or tulip, the first robin and humming-bird, the first energies of spring. I learned to endure, and to be patient.

I learned, too, that in all things you must be obedient — obedient to your faith, to your family, to your con-science, to your work. Even when things are demanded of you which you believe to be unfair, never do less than the best you can. When necessary I would ride three miles through freezing rain to deliver one paper. Try to give more than merely what is required of you.

Sometimes the fruit of your labors will vanish through no fault of your own. When I was fifteen my father had a pressing financial need and I brought out all my savings and gave it to him. I don't think of my labors as wasted. Every experience is education, every coincidence is valu-able. Hard as my paper route was, to buy my mother a birthday present with my own money or give my little sis-ter a day at the fair was rewarding for me. Digging a little deeper to help someone who had less came back to me tenfold.

Like love, respect and devotion to creation cannot be exhausted but returns to you in countless ways. The more you tend and care for natural treasures the more you'll experience their value in your sense of aliveness. When we glorify the Creator, we must give back a little of what we receive. This isn't difficult to do. Plant a tree, pick up trash, build a bluebird nesting box, plant a butterfly bush; there are hundreds of choices and opportunities. Be sensitive to nature, to plants, to animals — they suffer, too.

I cannot say this enough: So much depends on attitude, on your world view. You can choose to see life as unremarkable, an ordinary process of living and dying, and all creation a coincidental evolutionary happening; or you can choose to perceive something divine in the spirit of life and in its manifestations, you can choose to have an eye that truly sees, an ear that hears.

Years ago I was walking in our woods when I observed with disappointment several dying or dead tall pines. Their bark had slipped, many limbs had fallen, leaving only the decaying cambium inner core. How disheartening to someone who loves trees! But then some thoughts came to me which changed my viewpoint. I share them with you here.

> I saw a tree.
> Moribund, scoured white by wind and sun
> It flung its branches to the sky
> As if to cry, "Love me!
> Though I do not live, yet
> To birds and insects I refuge give."

# THE CREATION

My own inner poetry afforded me an attitude adjustment.

❧

On your great-great grandmother Lula's farm was a large bell sitting on top of a tall pole. All the farms had them. They were rung at appointed hours, such as dinnertime or quitting time. If a bell were sounded at an odd time it meant a fire or some other urgent matter. Farmers and farmhands dropped what they were doing and hurried to the call.

Only on a few occasions when it was time for farm workers to leave the fields or break for noontime shade was I able to satisfy my eagerness to ring the bell. A keen ear could pick up the chorus of bells sounding in the distance. The bells were mounted on tall cedar poles or high in trees. My thrill was not merely swinging on the rope to ring the bell, I was excited to be the one to send the signal to tired men that their day was over and they could come home at last.

The childhood days I spent on my grandmother's farm were for me the happiest times of my life. While I was there I had to employ a substitute to deliver my papers. This would be a boy to whom I had diligently taught my route. I would negotiate his pay — never as much as my own earnings, but perhaps two-thirds of it. Oh, at ten or eleven I was quite a businessman! But always I worried when I was away and had to rely on a substitute. I questioned his reliability, wondered if he would really pump all the way up the hills to the farthest houses, wondered if he would go at all. I could imagine my papers lying in an unopened bundle at Wynnton School, our pickup point, and customers angry at me.

On the farm I seldom went barefoot as other kids did. My feet were flat and I had funny-looking toes. I thought my feet were ugly. I was embarrassed by them. So mostly I wouldn't remove my shoes. Once when I did go barefoot I was climbing the rough wood slat barnyard fence when I slipped and drove a large splinter halfway through my little toe. My father had to remove it with pliers.

In contemporary America one wonders how many bells would have to be rung for a neighbor to rush to another's aid. Today people tend to do only that which pleases them. A nation in which every man looks only after himself is a nation in moral collapse. I fear you are entering an era when little is demanded of the individual, an age when if you choose not to work you are not chastised for slothfulness. We are becoming a socialistic society in which many believe they are entitled to food, shelter, medical care, education, even a certain level of luxury. It very well might be you who will work four or five days a week to provide not only food and shelter but cell phones and iPods for those who refuse to make their own way. I encourage you to be compassionate, but caution you never to destroy a man's dignity and sense of self-worth by giving him a free ride.

America is a remarkably responsive and generous

THE CREATION

country. Dozens of mission organizations prove that a great segment of our society believe in helping others. More than any other nation, we open our hearts to the damaged, the hungry, the unfortunate. Still, in our grandparents' childhood, a neighbor didn't lock his house against his neighbor. Today so tightly are doors barred it's doubtful one would even hear the urgent peal of a neighbor's bell.

I hope you will choose to be different. I don't mean throw caution to the wind, act irresponsibly or carelessly. But I hope you will not be afraid to get involved. Your forefathers took risks. They weren't only concerned with saving their own skins, but with serving the common good. They loved the earth, and everything it produced. They considered life a gift.

I believe the closer a person is to God's creations and to the love our Creator taught us, the less likely he is to be self-centered, greedy and materialistic. Human nature doesn't always highly rate treasures that are free. We tend to want what others want, to value what others value. We tend to be envious, and to allow that which attracts others to attract us. I sometimes wonder if we are victims of our own senses. Very likely the less our eyes perceive the less we desire. Think how blessed is the simple mind that places love of natural gifts above manmade ones!

All through life you will encounter those who appear not to have learned to love very deeply, even their own families. Your love for others should be developed and nurtured, and you can do this only if you resolve to do it. When you are led to the mates who'll share your lives, remember that people change, looks, circumstances, ideals, and tastes change; but those you choose to love should become part of yourselves, and this shouldn't be conditional. When you truly love someone you don't wish to change them, you value them for who they are and what they are. You don't try to control or manipulate them, you respect their space. To try to remake them to your own preferences simply means that you love yourself more than them.

It's natural that one day your hearts will go out to everyone and the next day you may try to hide within yourselves, speak as little as possible, and nurse your own dissatisfactions. On some days you will feel close to God and creation; on others you'll doubt the very foundation of your faith. Some days you will not like people at all. You'll find nothing about them that is lovable and attractive. Try to love them anyway. Remember that even with an attitude of faith, hope, optimism and gratitude, days will come when you feel neither loving nor lovable. On such days don't give up. Love demands courage and very often separation from others. Love the world not for what it can give you but for the privilege of being a part of it and giving something back to it.

More eloquent than I could be, Elizabeth Barrett Browning said it this way:

# THE CREATION

Earth's crammed with heaven,
And every common bush afire with God;
But only he who sees, takes off his shoes,
The rest sit round it and pluck blackberries . . .

⚜

During your mother's childhood one of the things that pleased her most was "making a middle." She would carefully arrange blocks, butter tubs or toys in a circle or in the shape of rooms, then install herself in the center. And in her middle, she felt secure. Perhaps it was a sense of having a wall between her and the world. Perhaps it was memory of the all-encompassing womb. Whatever the attraction, her middle was her childlike expression of her need for protectiveness.

As she grew older she began to believe that, along with her parents, her "middle" was her faith. This shield of protection was not made of visible blocks and things but one she carried with her at all times, in all places. Still, it's important to understand that no spiritual conviction can entirely shield one from pain. During her youth she wept many times over some injustice or slight. And before she met your father she experienced broken relationships, which are always painful. Such experiences hurt deeply, yet from them we learn about character, about people, and especially about what we want in our lives.

For your mother, making a middle was a wonderful

childhood game. But I ask you to consider making your middle, deciding how it will be constructed and who will be the center of it.

I wish I could take you back to the time when Americans instinctively reached out to their neighbors, when they would do everything they could to return something found, when sitting by a fire or taking a drive were the kinds of things families did together. I wish I could take you back to the times when schoolchildren said the Lord's Prayer and the Pledge of Allegiance in classrooms, when prayer opened high school football games, when to hold a girl's hand during a prom was all a boy hoped for, when tears came into one's eyes when singing "America the Beautiful," when a student wouldn't dare show disrespect for a teacher and teachers loved watching young minds grow, when honesty

and sympathy toward one another was the norm instead of the unique, and when we knew America was great, would fight anyone who said it wasn't, stood proudly under her flag and never doubted that if we were lost somewhere in the world, America would come for us.

This America was quite different from the one in which you will grow up, when a teacher can be put in jail for uttering a prayer, when people are thrilled to watch a film of a young girl or boy enduring a beating by half a dozen adversaries, when lying and cheating is the norm instead of the exception, when not only doors but hearts are locked, when both God and patriotism are obsolete, and when love for one another, especially for a stranger, is considered impossibly naïve.

How I wish I could protect you from a morally teetering nation, from the persecution you'll suffer if you believe in God and all He taught, from the slow decay of national liberty. How I wish I could tell you to look into your soul and spirit for the Light of the World, not the hateful and atheistic babbling of those who believe man is created only to get all he can out of the world, then to die.

Still, despite all its warts and blemishes, America is the greatest republic and the most successful experiment in freedom ever attempted. A nation which allows its citizens to desecrate its flag and spew hatred against it is a free nation indeed. The original thirteen colonies, of which Georgia is one, brought together a central government with limited and restrained powers. Today the powers of this government and the abuse of individual freedom is eroding our democracy as a great flood sweeps away the pilings beneath a strong bridge. But voices of those who still believe in a free republic will never be totally extinguished. There is no force on earth that can obliterate our personal faith or our love for God and for the land. We love our beautiful country and must not lose heart.

I encourage you to choose your lifestyles carefully — what you will do, what you will be, whose company you keep. The importance of how you use your talents, your time and resources, and what you do for others, cannot be underrated. But I believe who you are, who you choose to be, is more significant than what you do. Education, intelligence, economy, circumstances play a big part in what we can and cannot accomplish. But the will to be what one resolves to be comes not from without but from within. The I will of your life is more critical than all the possibilities wealth and circumstances can offer.

Never say you will do something and not do it. Remember, your word is not measured by degrees. It is either true or it is not. A promise to help a friend in his yard is no less crucial than the promise to pay a financial obligation. Guard your word as though it's the most valuable possession you have. Establish for yourself a reputation as someone who does what he says he will do. If you falter, don't make excuses, don't gloss over anything. Let integrity become a habit.

I hope the greatness of our democracy will survive

your generation. It will be up to you to help it survive. To speak up when you see an injustice, to try to make the world a little better place, to contribute to the love of creation and to the good of others, to be a small individual beacon of love — I hope this will be your legacy.

Whatever one chooses to believe about the origin of life, without faith in the dignity and worth of man, and in caring for every individual as Jesus taught us, mankind is doomed. And whatever you face, I believe the troubles in life are not nearly so painful if you have learned to love those people, blessings and creative gifts which you have chosen to bring into your life.

With God's guidance it will be up to you to find your way. You will be led by the love which has made footprints for you to follow long after those who made them are gone.

One footprint I hope you can follow is this: try your best to hold your tongue. Learn to speak little and listen much. Don't articulate every thought, every argument, every spiteful response that comes into your heads. Try to be sensitive to the feelings of others. Remember that people will do and say things they don't really mean. Try not to hurt anyone, especially in order to get even. No matter how ugly or mean someone is to you, lashing out is no remedy. Make every effort not to hurt another heart and your own heart stands less chance of getting hurt. When someone else speaks show them the courtesy of letting them finish. Don't interrupt. Learn to listen and to be open to others.

During times of your greatest success, never fail to be humble. Humility is a gift but it must be nurtured. Remember that your life is not entirely your own. It, too, is a gift. Be a strong leader, take a positive stance, but at all times reject arrogance and pride.

And learn to marshal your forces. I'm convinced the average individual can accomplish as much in one day as most do in two. By responsible planning and utilizing the people and resources available to you, you can achieve far more than you imagined. Time is valuable, your thoughts, your contributions are valuable. Don't waste them.

I wish that I could leave you another footprint: never be cheap or stingy. Don't love money. Respect it for what it can do, protect it for something that is hard to gather. But never forget the things it cannot do. Selfishness and a love of money is simple poison to the joyful spirit.

Remember that your body is yours and yours alone. If you listen, it won't lie to you. Do not in turn use it to lie. Don't deceive others for your own pleasure, but never be ashamed of your body. It is intricately and wonderfully made. You'll be surrounded by young men and women who live for the flesh. Nothing is too shocking for them, nothing is sacred. They use their physical bodies for barter, for currency. The danger is that eventually there will remain for them no excitement, no hidden treasure, no special gift.

I don't know why the makers of movies and pop music and books seek to fill our eyes and ears with contempt for individual worth. I understand that they are expressing themselves through "art." I understand that cruelty, masochism and promiscuity have always been with us. But how the torn and bleeding and tortured body is supposed to be entertaining I cannot fathom. Whatever disciples of brutality others may be, you can choose to respect the temple over which you have ultimate authority.

I had no doubt that the urgent call I felt at age fourteen to be a significant voice in the world, to have influence on the way people thought and felt, was from God, and I pursued it passionately. But at sixteen, my father became seriously ill and I inherited a family of four. I accepted this responsibility, remembering that I must honor my father and mother. I had to become the father of the family. To finish school, work one-hundred-hour weeks, care for a family, and try to pursue my vision became an impossibly demanding and stressful task. I started a business, but since I had no experience and had never worked for anyone, I had to teach myself everything — mistakes and inexperience cost years of failure. It was a lonely, fearful time. The key to this prison was money, and at last it came. I learned it was better to have it than not have it. I also learned how truly insignificant money is to the heart's joy. All the time I was living this life I was yearning for another. Business was a way to provide for a family of four, but I never forgot the angel's calling.

One obstacle after another fell into my path. At times I lost my bearing. I felt fate was against me. I doubted God, I doubted my own worth. I disliked the man that bitter disappointment sometimes made me. I said and wrote things I wasn't proud of. I didn't want to live an ordinary life. I was angry with God for encouraging such noble ideals only to allow the cruel ironies of fate to assault me on every front. I learned perseverance and patience but despite my determination to love people I left enemies in my wake.

Why do I tell you this? Because if ever you feel a special calling I encourage you to pursue it faithfully. But I have learned that not everyone is meant to shape the future of mankind. Our lives are worthwhile if we touch only one or two other lives. No ambition, not even the noblest one, should consume us. Being a good mother, a good husband or father, showing the face of strong moral character — in this way, in your own small circle, you can make a difference.

Everyone has a gift. Some may be good at building, some at solving mathematical problems, some may paint or write, some may sing or teach, others may have the gift of compassion or of leadership. Try not to delay in discovering your gifts, and when you do pursue them vig-orously. Make your best use of them. Above all, don't envy the gifts of others. Yours are yours. Do the best you can, not to glorify yourselves but rather those whose lives you touch.

Not a single talent goes unnoticed. Every gift has value. The fruit of the spirit, love, joy, peace, patience, kindness, gentleness, goodness, faithfulness, self-control — these, too, are gifts to be used and shared, the rewards of a giving heart.

Never give up on your dreams, have faith in them, per-severe against all odds. But do not let them drown you. There is no more honorable aspiration than to learn to live day by day and to seize each day's opportunity and blessing, however large or small.

And try not to live entirely in the future. Try not to base your joy on circumstances or relationships that you expect to come. I know it doesn't seem so to you now but life rushes by quickly. We tend to think if we can just achieve a certain goal our lives will be smooth sailing. But seldom does success bring the peace we believe it will bring. Quite often it only brings deeper and more urgent ambition. Human nature is restless. We're determined to climb mountains but often are not satisfied when we reach the top. We merely look across at other mountains and wonder what we might find there.

If there is anything I would like to pour into your hearts it is this: don't waste your lives. Treasure and enjoy every phase — youth, young adulthood, middle age, old age. Making joy and happiness conditional is a waste of your life. No matter what you hope to achieve, weigh carefully what you may have to sacrifice to get there.

You must look into yourselves, the spirit in you — not the world, not those around you — to find joy, but this won't come naturally. You must make up your minds to do it, and in this respect you will separate yourselves from the world while at the same time giving the world the best of yourselves to help make it a better place.

Our ancestors were farmers, teachers, clerks, businessmen, bankers, artists, thinkers, doers. Probably some were mean-spirited, blasphemous, greedy, ignoble. But they loved their country.

Your great-grandmother Wylma was a woman whose vision and intelligence reached beyond her circumstances and her economic limits. Her formal education was brief. Her circle was small, her opportunities insufficient. Her financial burdens were suffocating. As a result she was compelled to resign herself to a mundane life which otherwise might have been more rewarding to herself and to others. She was sensitive and forgiving, and I believe could have ascended intellectual and creative heights given the chance.

I believe you would have liked her. I know she would

have loved you. Love of her children and grandchildren was a major part of her life. She was a terrific cook and always remembered the things we liked (my favorite was banana pudding). She enjoyed fishing, she and your great-grandfather Cecil looked forward to nothing more than going out to their little lake. Once they stumbled into a wasps' nest and Wylma received over fifty stings. She went to the hospital for shots, but hardly complained, hardly even mentioned it.

She was a shy person — always worried about people behind her looking at the back of her hair. For someone of limited education she was smart, probably because she almost always had a book in her hand. She was a brave woman, too. After my father died, she lived alone for another fifteen years without fear in her big house. I know she was lonely. When she passed away she had thousands of slides of her grandchildren, of flowers, of mountains and fall leaves — she loved nature and everything of natural beauty.

Your great-grandfather Cecil had a small hardware store which never made money. He was a fixer. Almost never was a repairman called to our house, though the appearance of some of his work left much to be desired. My mother was a perfectionist. She would rip apart a whole dress or blanket if she discovered one dropped stitch. She found much to dislike about some of my father's handwork, but accepted it as the best he could do. The year he died he was trying to build a one-man motorized cart that would transport him across the woods and fields of their country place. This was before the popularity of the all-terrain vehicles. He mounted a motor on a frame, installed pulleys and gears, controls, a seat and a steering mechanism. After his death, this clumsy invention, like so many things, went into the trash bin of memory and optimism.

I wish I could bring your great-grandparents back. Seldom do we realize what we have until it's gone. Would I provide my father with an all-terrain vehicle? Of course. Would it be the best idea? Probably not. It would have taken away his inventiveness and most of all his determination to stay busy. It was in his genes to work, to build, to live an industrious and active life. It was to my parents the American way.

I had taken care of my mother and father and young sister since his near-death illness when I was sixteen. I realize now what a privilege this was, but during those hard years there were times when I couldn't understand why God placed such a burden on me. I had missed youth and young manhood, and was no stranger to depression, frustration and confusion. My faith was attacked mercilessly. My spirit burned with unfulfilled desires.

If we could only learn that life is not all about us we would be liberated from so much selfishness and envy and jealousy our hearts would be free to soar. So once again I reiterate these things which seem to me a world view which I hope will be a light to you:

Count your blessings. Almost always, no matter how

dire the circumstances, the good things in your lives will outweigh the bad.

Practice kindness and compassion. This will cost you no more than an extra moment, an extra word or gesture. Remember that kindness is a gift, and every gift comes back to the giver.

Savor every small and large joy. Whether it is in the bloom of a flower, the birth of a baby, or the smile of a stranger, decide to find happiness in little things that come to you. Your great-grandmother Thelma was a master of this. Her appreciation of small things gave her a sweet, peaceful and always hopeful disposition.

Be grateful for every favor. Express gratitude to those who bless you and those who bless others. It's not always things people do for you that count, it is the time and love and resources they give to others as well.

Try to develop one or two close friends. Remember to laugh and play with them, and to console. Real friendship demands self-sacrifice, putting another ahead of your own self-interests. Protect your friends fervently.

Learn to forgive not only those who seek forgiveness. Learn to forgive circumstances, disappointments, and learn to forgive yourselves. The past is always past. It cannot be changed, only your attitude toward what has happened can be changed. Forgiveness for a wrong, whether at the hands of man or of life itself, is to a great extent part of freeing yourselves from remorse.

Before a down day comes, develop strategies for

coping with them. Against those days of moodiness or depression, pre-plan remedies — time with someone you enjoy, an activity that brings you pleasure, even just a positive thought or hope. Marshal your good forces before the down days come.

Always try to be sensitive — to others, to animals and nature and plants. Always know that it is okay to cry. Allow your hearts to be touched. Usually, you can see your enemy's point of view. Forgive and sympathize. I believe sensitivity to the disappointments and hurts and sadness of others softens our own hearts and opens them to the gratitude and joys we might otherwise never perceive.

Never bully and hurt anyone. Children especially can be cruel. Perhaps it's a tool of the ego to cut others down so that we might feel superior to them. There appears no age restriction to the tendency toward a certain level of cruelty. What good is it to hurt others, even your enemy? Boyfriends and girlfriends try to inflict pain on each other when their relationships have ended. Mothers try to inflict pain on people who have hurt their children. But to what end? It's never easy to turn the other cheek, walk the extra mile. I caution you that breaking another's heart might provide a moment of vindication, but the satisfaction is short-lived. Hurtfulness comes back to damage our own hearts.

No matter how life or others might attack you, never give up. Never give up on your work or your aspirations, especially never give up on your convictions. It's all right to fail. This is not giving up. To fail one must first have tried. Don't admit defeat until you have done your best. Whatever odds you face, keep on. There is a difference between recognizing legitimate failure and quitting.

As a small child your mother was a determined little thing. When she made up her mind about something she was going to have it. Adult reasoning carried no weight. She could be stubborn and hardheaded. When she was unable to tie her shoelaces she would screw up her mouth and bang her head on the floor. If her mother were trying to put on something she didn't want to wear she would stiffen her arms and legs like an iron man. She knew how to wear me down, too. She would screw her face up into a horrendous contortion and wheeze, "Pl-e-e-a-se!" She wanted the last word, she wanted her way, but when she knew she had to give up she let it go.

Aggravating as this sometimes was, her determination was admirable. In its proper place persistence can be a valuable asset. Nothing should be attempted half-heartedly. Over and over you will hear this: If a thing is worth doing, it's worth doing well. Your level of ability and talent may be less than another's. Don't judge yourselves by them. Do your best, do not give up, and accept defeat with dignity.

A wonderful proverb is "Look before you leap." You'll spare yourselves much misery if you do nothing, say nothing, reveal nothing you aren't willing for God and the world to see. You never know what the future holds for you. Don't put yourselves in a compromising position which years later may come back to haunt you.

And develop strong self-reliance. Whenever a task has been set before you, count on yourselves and yourselves alone to do it. I have learned that we can manage with two hands when three are needed. Self-reliance means you'll muster resources and find ways to do things without relying on the reinforcement of others. It doesn't mean you'll never join forces with your marriage partner, your friend, your fellow worker, but only that you should pursue an idea, an ambition, a job as though you alone can do it. Then when help in any form comes you count this as an added blessing. Let yourselves be supported by love, faith and good works, not by the concept that anyone else could or should do your task for you.

Never cheat, steal, bully or betray a confidence. Such actions can only bring harm to you.

One afternoon when your mother was just beginning to walk she was on the floor investigating a vacuum cleaner. She accidentally pushed the switch and the machine roared into life. I was reading on the sofa not far away. Terrified, she clambered to her feet and ran to me as fast as her little legs could bring her — me, her father and protector. My heart still breaks whenever I think of that day.

Despite my hopes and my vision the birth of a child worked a transforming love. Ambition and ideals became secondary. To nurture and protect and love our children became more important than anything else. I believe the love of parents for their children and grandchildren assumes a special life of its own. I realize not every parent or grandparent feels this way. Some don't really want to be bothered; especially they don't want demands made on their time. But the love I speak of, God's beautiful gift of creation, redirects priorities and displaces our material aspiration with the awakening of an inner elevating being. It is a love which doesn't preclude other elements of life but which above all others will enable you to make sacrifices. Someday I hope you will have children and understand this better.

I wonder if love isn't an actual planned event of creation. Evolutionists tell us that man evolved over millions of years from the most primitive life form; that conscience, intellect, and reason are functions of the human brain. How, then, do certain elements of humanness appear to bypass the brain and go straight to the soul? It occurs to me that love of our Creator, of one another, of special people in our lives might be the single most significant gift of creation. The simplest minds can experience it. It is an element that reaches beyond the intellect, beyond reasoning, to a spiritual depth that all men do not have naturally; yet the capacity for love is born in every individual, and I don't believe it is the product of an evolutionary process.

Ambition and ideals are commendable. I encourage you to develop them and seek them vigorously. But these should be part of your journey, not your destination. As you gaze out the window, don't miss the gardens, the fruit, the bounty of creation you are passing by. Life is but the flicker of a candle. It is important that you live your days as they come, remembering that almost no earthly goal we choose is worth missing out on the life we are given to live. At times living each day will be painful, it will demand choices you would prefer not to make. As long as you are true to yourself and your convictions, even on the hard days you'll be living your life now, not in the future.

There is much to be serious about, much to be unsettled about. But it's better to focus on the reaffirming joys of life. You must make a decision about the attitude you'll practice. The desire to improve your lives, to get ahead, to make a contribution, even to change the future of mankind is admirable. But the desire for things — money,

possessions, power, position — is always a source of incurable unrest. Try to be satisfied with what you have. Try not to envy what others have. Try to devote some part of your time, your talent, your resources, to helping others. Enjoy each day as though it's your last day on earth. Don't compare what you have — your looks, your talent, your popularity, your position — with others. Remember that every blessing is a gift. Remain humble and grateful.

To be honest, the things I have spoken to you about are the principles and beliefs I have learned but failed miserably to practice. Could I go back and begin again I would try my best to embrace this view of life. My years could have been more peaceful and fruitful. I hope you are spared some of my disappointments and struggles, and that these thoughts may help you find joy in life. No matter how others might ridicule and persecute you, remember that our Creator asks no more of us than to love Him and to love each other.

When one makes up his mind to be happy with what he has, where he lives, and in the time he lives, changes he wishes to make become a journey whose destination is the joy of the spirit. The fear, the heartache, the pain, the humiliation, the disillusion, the sorrow will inevitably come. We can neither escape these nor avoid the damage they do to our hearts. But remember that your bodies are precious, your minds are a gift, your choices are your own, God loves you, and that more important than any earthly condition is the spirit of love which He has given you.

# A LETTER

I'm thankful for the privilege of making some small contribution to forming and shaping your lives. I hope that the principles of honesty, generosity, compassion, patience, and responsibility won't fail you. I pray for the individuals you may choose to become. I pray that you and your children and your children's children will live joyous and fruitful lives. I hope that in some small way I have been a light on your paths, and left footprints for you to follow. This I know: my love for you will go on . . . and on . . .

I love you,
Grandonald